Anne Frank

Angela Bull

Illustrated by
Stephen Gulbis

Hamish Hamilton
London

Titles in the Profiles *series*

Edith Cavell	0-241-11479-9	Montgomery of Alamein	0-241-11562-0
Marie Curie	0-241-11741-0	The Queen Mother	0-241-11030-0
Roald Dahl	0-241-11043-2	Florence Nightingale	0-241-11477-2
Thomas Edison	0-241-10713-X	Emmeline Pankhurst	0-241-11478-0
Anne Frank	0-241-11294-X	Pope John Paul II	0-241-10711-3
Elizabeth Fry	0-241-12084-5	Anna Pavlova	0-241-10481-5
Indira Gandhi	0-241-11772-0	Prince Philip	0-241-11167-6
Gandhi	0-241-11166-8	Beatrix Potter	0-241-12051-9
Basil Hume	0-241-11204-4	Lucinda Prior-Palmer	0-241-10710-5
Amy Johnson	0-241-12317-8	Viv Richards	0-241-12046-2
Helen Keller	0-241-11295-8	Barry Sheene	0-241-10851-9
John Lennon	0-241-11561-2	Mother Teresa	0-241-10933-7
Martin Luther King	0-241-10931-0	Queen Victoria	0-241-10480-7
Nelson Mandela	0-241-11913-8	The Princess of Wales	0-241-11740-2
Bob Marley	0-241-11476-4		

HAMISH HAMILTON CHILDREN'S BOOKS

Penguin Books Ltd, 27 Wrights Lane, London W8 5TZ (Publishing & Editorial)
and Harmondsworth, Middlesex, England (Distribution & Warehouse)
Viking Penguin Inc., 40 West 23rd Street, New York, New York 10010, U.S.A.
Penguin Books Australia Ltd, Ringwood, Victoria, Australia
Penguin Books Canada Limited, 2801 John Street, Markham, Ontario, Canada L3R 1B4
Penguin Books (N.Z.) Ltd, 182–190 Wairau Road, Auckland 10, New Zealand

First published in Great Britain 1984 by
Hamish Hamilton Children's Books

Copyright © 1984 text by Angela Bull
Copyright © 1984 illustrations by Stephen Gulbis

Reprinted 1985, 1986, 1987

British Library Cataloguing in Publication Data

Bull, Angela
Anne Frank. — (Profiles)
1. Frank, Anne — Juvenile literature   2. Jews —
Netherlands — Biography — Juvenile literature
I. Title   II. Series
940.53'15'03924   D810.J4

ISBN 0-241-11294-X

Typeset by Pioneer
Printed in Great Britain at the
University Press, Cambridge

Contents

1 THE PAPERS ON THE FLOOR 9

2 THE WORLD TURNED UPSIDE DOWN 15

3 THE SECRET ANNEXE 20

4 FEARS AND FRUSTRATIONS 27

5 MISUNDERSTOOD 32

6 DAY BY DAY 37

7 I WANT TO WRITE 42

8 PETER 46

9 INWARD COMPENSATIONS 50

10 NOT FORGOTTEN 55

Dutch memorial statue of Anne

1   The Papers on the Floor

'Are these all the valuables?' the German sergeant demanded.

The Dutch plain clothes policeman nodded. He laid a cashbox and some small trinkets on the table.

The sergeant glanced round the attic room, with its clutter of furniture, and its thin curtains pinned across the window. For a hiding place it was not too uncomfortable. There, and in four tiny interconnecting rooms, a group of eight Jews had been living concealed, until the Nazi patrol discovered them.

On the floor lay a briefcase. The sergeant picked it up, and shook out the contents — some notebooks, and a handful of papers. He peered at them closely. They might contain sabotage plans, or lists of other addresses where enemies of the German nation were hiding.

But no. He flicked through the pages with mounting contempt. Adolescent twitterings about Mummy and Daddy, outpourings about the sky and a chestnut tree, stories about elves — clearly it was all rubbish. He tossed the papers onto the floor, and put the cashbox and trinkets into the briefcase.

When the hiding place had been thoroughly searched, the prisoners were led downstairs, and out through the secret door. They walked quietly, as pale as ghosts, too shocked to resist. In the Amsterdam street, between the tall old house and the quiet canal, a police van was waiting. They climbed into the back, and away it drove, along the canal and over the bridge, towards the Gestapo headquarters.

The German sergeant was satisfied with his day's work. There was nothing of value left in the hiding place; he was sure of that.

But he was wrong. He had left the most valuable things of all, lying on the floor.

For a few days, the old house by the Amsterdam canal stood silent and empty. Then, gradually, life began to return. A cleaner was sent in to clear up the mess. Two secretaries, Miep Van Santen and Elli Vossen, climbed with trembling knees to their first floor office.

The ground floor was a warehouse, and above it were the offices of a firm of spice merchants. The building ran back a long way from the street, with a network of staircases, and rooms opening out of each other. And, behind a bookcase filled with box files, a low doorway led to the 'Secret Annexe', where eight people had lived in hiding for two years.

The cleaner moved through the Secret Annexe, sweeping up the debris. When he came to the little pile of papers, he paused. Then he gathered them up, and clattered down to the office.

'What are these papers?' he asked.

Miep and Elli stared at them in silence. They instantly recognized the small, neat writing, with its firm, slanting strokes. But as long as the Germans remained in Holland, it was safest to say nothing. If they betrayed any knowledge of the Secret Annexe, they might be arrested too. They shook their heads; and the cleaner laid the papers down, and returned to his work.

As soon as he had gone, the two women sprang up. Elli was twenty-five, and still in a flutter of nerves from the German raid. Miep was older and steadier, an Austrian married to a Dutchman. Together they examined the notebooks.

The dated entries showed plainly that this was a diary. The writing told them that it had been kept by Anne Frank, a girl of fifteen, the youngest and liveliest inhabitant of the Secret Annexe.

They turned the pages, until they reached the last entry.

'I keep on trying to find a way of becoming what I would so like to be, and what I could be — if there weren't any other people in the world.'

What exactly she had meant, Miep and Elli did not know.

'We must keep it safe,' said Miep. 'Anne might come back.'

But Elli shook her head. Was it likely that a Jewish girl, taken away by the Nazis, would ever return?

For this was August 1944, and although the British and American armies had landed in France, and were moving eastwards across Europe, Holland was still in the grip of Hitler; and Hitler, the tyrannical ruler of Germany, had decreed that all the Jews in Europe must

Hitler

die. That was why a teenage girl, who had never in her life harmed anyone, had been dragged away to a concentration camp, and almost certain death.

Why did Hitler hate the Jews so much? It was a complicated question, with many different answers. As a penniless young man, trying to scrounge a living in Vienna, the capital of Austria, he had watched the powerful Austrian Jews, and writhed with bitterness and envy. In the First World War he had fought in the German army, and suffered the humiliation of defeat. The downfall of Germany, he decided, was the fault of the Jewish bankers and industrialists. They had failed to supply enough arms. They must be punished.

The Russian ruler, the Czar, had also been over-thrown. His enemies, the Communists, had been inspired by a Jewish writer called Karl Marx. It seemed to Hitler's crazed logic that, whenever Jews had a hand in things, disaster followed.

If Hitler alone had had such ideas, there might have been no danger to the Jews. But many Germans, besides minority groups in other countries, shared his views. For hundreds of years the Jewish people, with no country of their own, had been scattered across Europe, leading separate lives among other populations. Because they had their own religion, their own customs, even their own way of dressing, they were never absorbed into their host countries. They stood out; they were different. To many Christians they seemed to bear a terrible guilt as the people who had murdered Jesus. As Pontius Pilate washed his hands of the responsibility for Jesus's death, the Jewish leaders had cried — 'His blood be on us, and on our children.' All through the centuries after Christ, there had been times when Christians turned on Jews, and massacred them in revenge for the Crucifixion.

To Hitler it was an outrage that Jews should live in Germany. He believed that the Germans were unique, a master race, destined to rule the world. The Jews had no place amongst them. They must be exterminated.

As soon as Hitler came to power, he turned his hatred into action. He made laws against the Jews. They could not hold important positions. Their shops were boycotted. They could no longer expect police protection if they were attacked. Presently some were

Anne in May 1938

sent to concentration camps, to work as slaves, or die. As the Second World War began, and the German armies overran Europe, the same laws were spread. Jews could not go out in the evenings. They could not use parks, or swimming pools, or public transport. And so that there was no mistake about their identity, they were forced to wear, as a badge, a six-pointed yellow star, with the word 'Jew' on it.

Once the Jews were identified, it was easy to get rid of them. They could be picked up by the police, and dispatched to hideous, unknown destinations. That was why Anne Frank and her family, who were Jews, had gone into hiding, in the old house beside the Amsterdam canal.

2 The World Turned Upside Down

Anne Frank was born on June 12th 1929 at Frankfurt, in Germany. Her parents both belonged to wealthy German families. Poor and hunted though they became, always, at the back of their minds, were memories of their youth, when they had gone to balls and parties, when Mrs Frank had worn elegant clothes, and Mr Frank had danced with beautiful girls.

But besides being rich, they were Jewish; and so, when Hitler came to power, the Franks fled to Holland, taking their two little daughters, Margot and Anne. They chose to settle in Amsterdam, where many Jews were already living. Mr Frank established himself in business. They found a comfortable house, and a good school for the girls. In these new surroundings they hoped to resume the pleasant way of life they had enjoyed before.

Margot was four years older than Anne. She was gentle, intelligent, and very good. Anne loved her dearly, but sometimes she wished that Margot was not quite so perfect.

Anne was pretty, lively — and far from perfect. She too was clever, but because she spent so much time gossiping and joking, she never got such high marks as

Margot. 'Mrs Chatterbox' was her school nickname. She was like quicksilver, one moment entertaining the class with her tricks and cheeky answers, the next lost in a daydream. Naughty though she was, the teachers always liked her. She had dozens of girl friends, and boys swarmed round her like bees round a honeypot, begging to cycle home with her, or take her for walks. They amused her, but only one boy really counted, Peter Wessel, who was older than she was, and kept aloof from her crowd of admirers.

Yet, surprisingly, Anne often felt lonely. All her family and friends seemed content to skim the surface of life. Anne wanted somebody to share the deep thoughts and feelings which, behind all her gaiety, secretly absorbed her. But there was no-one; and so she began to invent for herself another friend, a special friend, a girl called Kitty.

June 12th 1942 was Anne's thirteenth birthday; and amongst her piles of presents — books, chocolates, games and money — she found a fat, stiff-covered notebook. Immediately she knew how she would use it. It would be a diary; and because she would confide in it the things she would only tell a special friend, she would pretend each entry was a letter. She would begin 'Dear Kitty', and end 'Yours, Anne'.

There was plenty to say. By now the peace which the Franks had found in Amsterdam had been shattered. In 1940 the Germans had invaded Holland, and the persecutions which had driven Anne's family to flight seven years earlier, overtook them again. In Holland, as in Germany, the Jews were Hitler's chosen victims.

16

Wearing a yellow star in occupied Amsterdam, 1942

Conspicuous in their yellow star badges, they were forced to submit to the old horrors; to the limited freedom, the humiliations, and the knowledge that, if they did not submit, there would be no mercy.

At first Anne hardly noticed what was happening. Of course the restrictions were annoying, but she was much more interested in school, in her collection of film star photographs, and in her new boy friend, Harry. She terrified her parents by thoughtlessly staying out late; Jews had to be in by eight o'clock.

Less than a month after she had begun the diary, Mr Frank told Anne that they might have to go into hiding. Life was becoming very frightening. Because he was a Jew, Mr Frank had been made to give up his

17

business. He handed it over to his two Dutch partners. Now the Franks were much poorer. They had to take a lodger to make ends meet. But far worse than that, Jews — even Jews who kept the rules — were being arrested, and sent to concentration camps.

In wartime conditions it was impossible to escape from Holland; and so, for more than a year, the Franks had been preparing a hiding place. Clothes, furniture, and tinned food were stocked there. 'Make the most of your carefree young life while you can', (1) Mr Frank warned Anne. It would not last much longer.

Three days after his warning, 'the world,' Anne told Kitty, 'turned upside down.' (2)

She was spending a lazy Sunday afternoon, reading and sun-bathing, when the doorbell rang, and an official letter was delivered. 'It's a call-up for Daddy', Margot whispered. Anne was horrified. A call-up almost certainly meant imprisonment in a concentration camp. The grown-ups consulted anxiously behind closed doors. Margot and Anne crept away to their bedroom. Suddenly Margot revealed that the call-up was not really for their father. She herself, a girl of only sixteen, was to be taken away. Anne burst into tears.

But she could not waste time crying; there was too much to be done. They must pack and leave before the Nazis came for Margot. Hurriedly, the girls began to fill their school satchels. Anne put her diary in first. Hairpins, handkerchiefs, books and old letters followed; 'the craziest things,' Anne wrote to Kitty, 'but memories mean more to me than dresses.' (3)

People from her father's business, it seemed, were

involved in their plans. Mr Frank's former secretary, Miep, and her husband, Henk, called and took away piles of clothes. The Franks wanted to pack more, but their lodger hovered round, and they dared not do anything to arouse his suspicions. Finally, exhausted with the strain, Anne tumbled into bed, and fell asleep.

At 5.30 next morning, her mother woke her. Hot though it was, Anne squeezed into all the remaining clothes she could manage — two vests, three pairs of pants, a dress with a skirt and jacket on top, a coat, two pairs of stockings, shoes, a woolly hat and a scarf. 'I was nearly stifled,' (4) she wrote; but Jews could not be seen carrying suitcases.

They ate a quick meal, scribbled a note for the lodger, and said good-bye to their cat, who would be looked after by neighbours. Then leaving the beds unmade, and the breakfast things unwashed, they slipped quietly out of their house.

'We only wanted to get away,' Anne wrote, 'only escape and arrive safely, nothing else.' (5)

Diary references
1. 5 July 1942
2. 8 July 1942
3. 8 July 1942
4. 8 July 1942
5. 8 July 1942

3   The Secret Annexe

Rain poured down as the Franks, smothered in layers of clothes, hurried through the streets. Jews were forbidden to use the buses; and people in cars, seeing the telltale yellow stars, dared not stop to offer them lifts.

Only now did Anne's parents tell her where they were going. They were to hide inside the old house where Mr Frank had had his office, and where his partners, Mr Kraler and Mr Koophuis, still worked. These two shared the Franks' secret, and so did the secretaries, Miep and Elli.

The tall, thin house, facing the Prinsengracht canal, was a perfect place for hiding. It was like a rabbit warren inside, with its interconnecting rooms, and dark, breakneck staircases. On the ground floor was a warehouse, managed by Elli's father, Mr Vossen. The offices were on the next floor, with storerooms above them; and from the second floor landing a steep staircase led to five tiny back rooms, also on two floors. This was the back wing where the Franks were to live. 'Although it leans to one side and is damp, you'd never find such a comfortable hiding place anywhere in Amsterdam,' [1] Anne wrote in her diary; and she drew

The office building in which Anne lived from 1942 to 1944

a plan so that Kitty could see exactly what it was like. She gave it a name too — the Secret Annexe.

But, coming in out of the rain that first Monday morning, it did not look very comfortable. The little rooms were crammed with boxes, and piles of bedding, stored away over the past few months. Dismayed by the confusion, and wretched at leaving their home, Mrs Frank and Margot gave way. They collapsed onto the unmade beds. But Anne and her father had more courage. Instead of collapsing, they were eager to get things straight.

Curtains were the first essential. If anyone looked out from the houses behind, and saw strange people in the disused wing, they might report them to the Nazis. Quickly Anne and Mr Frank tacked odd strips of material together, and pinned them over the windows. Then, feeling safer, they turned to the boxes. They worked all day, arranging furniture and filling drawers and cupboards. By nightfall the beds were made and the rooms were tidy.

Anne and Margot shared a tiny bedroom leading off the living-room, where their parents slept. It looked bleak, until Anne brightened it up by sticking postcards and film star photographs all over the walls. Next door was the bathroom. Upstairs was another small bedroom, and a larger room with a sink and cooker. These were reserved for another family.

For, since the Sunday when she had heard they were to hide, Anne had known that some other people were to join them, the Van Daans. Mr Van Daan, who was also a Jew, had been in business with Mr Frank. He and his wife, with their teenage son, Peter, and their cat, Mouschi, arrived in the Secret Annexe just a week after the Franks, and received a great welcome. At once it was decided that they would all share meals, and live as one large family.

The Van Daans brought interesting news. Early on the morning of the Franks' disappearance, their lodger, Mr Goudsmit, had telephoned Mr Van Daan in alarm. He had found the disordered breakfast table, and the note about the cat, and he could not understand what had happened. He begged Mr Van Daan to come round, which was just what Mr Van Daan was hoping for. He hurried to the house, and, according to a pre-arranged plan, 'discovered' an address jotted down on Mr Frank's writing pad. It was, he told Mr Goudsmit, the address of some friends of the Franks. They lived far away, in a town called Maastricht, and they had once promised to help the Franks. No doubt they had fetched them away in the night.

Mr Goudsmit swallowed the story, and so did the neighbours. One lady told Mr Van Daan that she had 'quite definitely' heard a car stop to pick up the Franks in the night. The Frank family sighed with relief. If the Nazis believed they had left Amsterdam, they would not trouble to search for them.

But clearly life, even in hiding, would be hazardous. A visitor to the office might find their staircase by chance. So Mr Kraler had a clever idea. He asked Mr Vossen, the warehouseman, to make a bookcase which fitted over the door at the staircase foot. It was hinged, so that it could swing back; but when it was

A swinging bookcase concealed the entrance

closed, and filled with box files, it looked like part of
the office furniture. Nobody could guess what it hid.

The swinging bookcase was only one of the ways in

which the hiders were helped by the kind office people. In her diary Anne called them 'the protectors'. Every day they brought food, which was cooked on the stove in the Van Daans' room. Food was rationed, so the protectors had to obtain false ration books, or buy from a few courageous shopkeepers, who knew that Jews were hiding in Amsterdam, and who risked their lives to supply them with food.

Without food, of course, the Franks and Van Daans could not have survived, but their protectors brought other things too. They provided clothes, books and newspapers. They lent a radio. Best of all, they simply dropped in to chat. Cooped up in their hiding place, the Franks and Van Daans often felt like prisoners who could not escape. The daily visits of their protectors helped them to feel less forgotten, more in touch with ordinary life as it was going on all the time, outside the walls of the old house by the Amsterdam canal.

Diary reference
1.   11 July 1942

Behind the bookcase

4 Fears and Frustrations

Once things were put straight, the hiding place was outwardly fairly comfortable. Mrs Frank and Mrs Van Daan tried to keep up the standards they were used to in their own homes. The families sat down formally to meals, with napkins on their laps, and proper soup plates for soup. Food, though dull, was plentiful. A hundred and fifty tins of vegetables had been stockpiled, and the protectors got them six large sacks of dried peas and beans. Peter dragged five of them up to the loft, but the sixth split, and dried beans showered down on Anne, who was standing below. After a moment's panic over the rattling of the falling beans, Peter began to laugh. Until then, Anne had rather despised him. She thought him a 'shy, gawky youth', [1] ridiculously attached to an old blue muffler, which he always wore. But when they shared a joke, she liked him better.

Another day they had fun making sausages. Wrapped in a butcher's apron, Mr Van Daan minced meat, stuffed skins, and strung sausages from the ceiling to dry. 'They looked frightfully funny', [2] Anne told Kitty.

Unfortunately such jolly moments were rare. Anne's diary shows that the Secret Annexe was not a happy place. The Franks and the Van Daans had been friendly enough in the past, when they had only met occasionally. In those days it had not mattered that the Franks were better educated, cooler, and more reserved than the outspoken, excitable Van Daans. Now that they were all shut up together, it mattered a great deal. They got on each other's nerves; and quarrels broke out which horrified Anne.

The mothers were mostly to blame. When disagreements arose, Mr Frank stayed calm and self-controlled, and Mr Van Daan could usually be soothed by a cigarette. But both Mrs Frank and Mrs Van Daan had sharp tongues, and whether they turned on their children, their husbands, or each other, they meant to be hurtful.

Mrs Van Daan was really German, like the Franks, and when she was angry, Anne wrote, she would 'reel off a lot of German . . . just like a coarse, red-faced fishwife.' [3] Mrs Frank would be either maddeningly superior, or give way to tears of self-pity.

'Why do grown-ups quarrel so easily, so much, and over such idiotic things?' [4] Anne wondered. It had never happened when they lived at home. Now she witnessed childish squabbles over who ate most, or washed up, or whose plates and sheets were used, varied by moans over beloved possessions left behind.

The reason was, of course, the strain of hiding. It was enough to change everyone's character; and they seemed to change for the worse. There were two particular causes of tension.

The first was simply being shut up. Through their

protectors and the radio, they kept, at least partly, in touch with the outside world; and at night they left the Secret Annexe, and wandered all over the old house. But during the day they had to keep absolutely still and quiet in their small rooms, never speaking above a whisper. One involuntary cough, heard by a visitor to the office, could betray them all. When a plumber spent three days working on the office pipes, the hiders could not even use the lavatory. 'Daddy and I improvised a pottie,' Anne told Kitty. 'I don't think that was nearly as bad as having to sit still and not talk . . . After being flattened by three days of continuous sitting, my bottom was stiff and painful.' (5)

One Sunday Anne and Margot crept into the front office with cans of hot water, to have a good wash. Through a slit in the curtain, they peeped at the world outside. They saw children playing, cyclists speeding along, and a houseboat on the canal, with a little dog barking on the deck. Anne choked back her envious longing to be outside too. 'I can't tell you how oppressive it is *never* to be able to go outdoors,' she wrote sadly; 'also I'm scared to death that we shall be discovered and shot.' (6)

That was the real cause of tension in the Secret Annexe. Under the quarrels, even under the jokes, they were all terrified. At an unexpected sound, every face turned white. Once the bookcase door stuck. The knocking they heard was only Mr Koophuis trying to get in, but, for a moment, the hiders were certain the Nazis had arrived. Another night, mysterious sounds downstairs threw them into a panic. Evidently a burglar

View of Prinsengracht Canal

had crept into the office, and he soon crept away again. But, fearing that he might return, the hiders dared not flush the lavatory; and as the tension affected everyone's stomachs, 'you can imagine what the atmosphere was like', (7) Anne told Kitty.

30

They knew only too well what their fate would be if they were caught. Newspapers, radio, and their protectors brought news of what was happening to other Jews in Holland. They were being driven away in cattle trucks and army lorries to the concentration camp at Westerbork. Families were separated. Some people were beaten. Most had their heads shaved. Finally they were sent on to camps in Germany. There 'they are murdered . . . gassed,' (8) Anne wrote. She heard that her best school friend, Lies Goossens, was among those who had been taken away.

Anne lay awake at night, haunted by fear, and by guilt because she was still safe. The only relief was to tell everything to Kitty. 'I get frightened when I think of close friends who have been delivered into the hands of the cruellest brutes that walk the earth,' she confessed. 'And all because they are Jews!' (9)

Diary references
1. 14 August 1942
2. 10 December 1942
3. 28 September 1942
4. 28 September 1942
5. 29 September 1942
6. 11 July 1942
7. 25 March 1943
8.   9 October 1942
9. 19 November 1942

5 Misunderstood

The grown-ups were far too preoccupied with their own worries to spare any sympathy for Anne. Indeed their main feeling about her seemed to be irritation.

The trouble was that Anne was too lively. At school she had always been full of jokes and laughter and mischief. That was why she had been so popular. Her last boy friend, Harry, had complimented her on the way she kept him awake. Shutting up a person like Anne in the Secret Annexe was like pouring lemonade into too small a bottle, and screwing the cap on too tightly. She fizzed and bubbled and threatened to explode — and she got on everyone's nerves.

Anne was the youngest of the hiders. Peter was fifteen, Margot was sixteen, and, compared with her, they seemed mature and sensible. Besides, Peter kept himself to himself, staying alone for hours in his slip of a bedroom, while Margot was too good and helpful ever to upset anybody. 'She is such a goody-goody, perfection itself, but I seem to have enough mischief in me for the two of us put together,' [1] Anne told Kitty crossly.

At meals Margot and Peter were silent, while Anne argued, and cheeked the grown-ups. She gave Mrs Van

Anne in May 1942

Daan the excuse for many a spiteful remark. 'Anne's so frightfully spoilt,' Mrs Van Daan would say. 'I wouldn't put up with it if Anne were my daughter.' (2) Then Anne's mother would be provoked into scolding her exasperating child, and Anne smarted under the reprimands and criticisms of the two women. Often she cried herself to sleep over the wounds they had inflicted on her. 'If I talk everyone thinks I'm showing off,' she moaned to Kitty; 'when I'm silent they think I'm ridiculous; rude if I answer, sly if I get a good idea, lazy when I'm tired, selfish if I eat a mouthful more than I should.' (3) They never seemed to reflect on how much she too had given up.

And it was very hard for Anne to sacrifice cheerfully her interests and pleasures, friends and freedom; and live, day after day, caged, silent and uncomplaining. The sudden change shook her nature to its core. She did not know how to adjust, and there was no-one to help her. Two years later, she could look back on herself, and understand. 'I was boisterous so as not to be miserable all the time,' (4) she wrote then. But in the first months her boisterousness rasped on the frayed nerves of the grown-ups. They snapped at her; and so the vicious circle of anger and misery went round and round.

Was it perhaps to punish her, that when another person came to join them in the Secret Annexe, Anne was condemned to share her room with him, while Margot moved cosily into the sitting-room where her parents slept?

The newcomer was a Jewish dentist, Dr Dussel. In November Miep contacted him, and offered him a hiding place. After a delay, while he fussily settled his patients and his accounts, he arrived at the old house by the canal; and was astonished, first by the swinging bookcase, and then by the sight of the Franks and Van Daans, waiting to welcome him with coffee and cognac.

'Didn't you escape then?' he gasped.

Forced into close quarters with him, Anne was, to begin with, prepared to be nice. But soon the old story was being repeated. She annoyed him, he spoke sharply, she retorted cheekily, and he flounced off to complain to her mother. Before long there were endless disagreements between them. He was always trying to keep her quiet. She could hardly turn over in bed without Dr Dussel whispering, 'Hush!' He liked to have the room to himself during the day, so Anne was turned out. Sometimes she longed to be alone, and

Margot Frank

there was nowhere to go. She fidgetted round the living-room, irritating everyone, especially her mother.

Anne's mother had never understood her. Gentle, obedient Margot, who gave not a moment's trouble, was always her favourite. Lively, impertinent Anne, she kept at arm's length. Anne knew how she felt, and minded dreadfully. Again and again, she struggled to get closer to her mother, to stir her into warmth and appreciation; and again and again she failed. Mrs Frank simply could not be the loving, sympathetic mother Anne longed for. She was too cool, too critical.

Anne's father was easier to get on with. 'Pim', as Anne called him, had a kindness and gentleness unique among the grown-ups in the Secret Annexe. Scoldings from him were rare. Generally he kept a little apart from the everyday troubles of the hiding place. Through the wearisome days, while the hiders had to be still and quiet, Pim lost himself in a book. Dickens was his favourite author, and he ploughed through the novels in English, with a dictionary by his side.

Anne longed to come first with Pim. Since her mother failed to understand her, she was always hoping that Pim would make amends by loving her best. But Pim had no idea how she felt. Sometimes he would be specially nice to Margot, and Anne burned with jealousy.

If it had not been for her diary, she might have broken down completely. The diary was her safety valve. She kept herself sane by pouring out her troubles to her dear, imaginary friend. 'Paper is patient,' [5] she wrote in one of her earliest entries. Now it proved far more patient than her mother, the Van Daans or Dr Dussel.

'Oh, so many things bubble up inside me as I lie in bed,' she told Kitty; 'having to put up with people I'm fed up with, who always misinterpret my intentions. That's why in the end I always come back to my diary. That is where I start and finish, because Kitty is always patient . . . Don't condemn me; remember that I too can sometimes reach bursting point.' [6]

Diary references
1. 27 September 1942
2. 27 September 1942
3. 30 January 1943
4.   5 May 1944
5. 20 June 1942
6.   7 November 1942

6 Day by Day

As the weeks and months passed by, and still the hiders were not discovered, life in the Secret Annexe settled into a routine. The quarrels continued, the weight of fear never lifted, but gradually the fears and quarrels were contained inside the orderly framework of each day.

At 6.45 the alarm clock rang, and, in turn, the hiders got up and used the bathroom. They all had to be dressed, with their beds made, before the warehousemen arrived at 8.30. These men were not in the secret, so, until the office staff came at 9.00, there had to be absolute silence; 'not a drop of water, no lavatory, no walking about, everything quiet,' [1] Anne wrote.

Once the office staff were moving about, it was safe for the hiders to move too, though always cautiously. They had breakfast — usually porridge — and then Anne settled down to a morning of school work. On her own she studied languages, history and mythology, and read everything the protectors could bring her. Buried in her books, she was able to forget her troubles for a while.

Lunch at 1.00 was a welcome break. The warehousemen went home, the protectors called in for a chat and sometimes a meal, and everyone listened to the news on the radio. Afterwards the grown-ups slept, but Anne read and studied again, and wrote her diary letters to Kitty.

At 5.30 the warehousemen finished work, and the hiders could relax. They left the Secret Annexe to walk about the old house. Mr Frank and Mr Van Daan read the business letters; the mothers cooked the supper; Anne peeped between the curtains at the desirable world outside. Sometimes she hardly knew how to bear her longing for a breath of fresh air.

Then it was supper, and everyone gathered round the table. This was a time for conversation, but, to Anne's despair, it turned all too readily into argument. The smallest differences of opinion could spark off a row between Mr and Mrs Van Daan, and they would storm at each other, while Pim sat tight-lipped, Mrs Frank looked superior, and Dr Dussel concentrated on the food. Margot and Peter seldom spoke, and Anne's head ached with the strain.

Arguments never lessened the Van Daans' appetites, but at last the meal, with its inevitable beans and potatoes and bread, was over. Preparations for bed began about 9 o'clock. 'Chairs are shoved about, beds are pulled down, blankets unfolded, nothing remains where it is during the day,' [2] Anne told Kitty. She herself slept on a divan so short that she had to put a chair on the end to lengthen it. After a precious interval of solitude in the bathroom, where she washed, curled her hair, and manicured her nails, she snuggled into the divan, hoping to fall asleep before Dr Dussel came creaking in.

Other things besides Dr Dussel disturbed Anne's nights. In the summer of 1943 there were British air raids on Amsterdam. Although Anne was glad that the Germans were being attacked, she was terrified of the bombs and guns. She flew into Pim's bed, and lay there shaking while the uproar lasted. None of the hiders knew what would happen to them if the house was bombed. Dutch people who lost their homes would be given shelter somewhere, but there could be no shelter for Jews. Anne huddled beside Pim, trembling, until the raids were over.

Apart from the air raids, and occasional scares over burglars, life was dreary and monotonous. The days passed with little change. Anne longed to enjoy the sort of fun she had had in the old days, but there was no fun in the Secret Annexe. 'I swallow valerian pills every day against worry and depression,' she told Kitty, 'but it doesn't prevent me being even more miserable the next day. A good hearty laugh would help more than ten valerian pills, but we've almost forgotten how to laugh.' [3]

Fun, fresh air, peace — there were so many things Anne wanted. All the hiders were the same. In one of her letters to Kitty, Anne described what everyone wished for most. Margot and Mr Van Daan longed to soak in deep, hot baths; Mrs Van Daan wanted a plate of cream cakes, and Mrs Frank a cup of good coffee; Pim thought he would like to go and visit Elli's father, Mr Vossen, who, to their dismay, had been admitted to hospital with cancer; Dr Dussel yearned to see his wife,

Edith Frank

who had been in England when the Germans invaded
Holland, and had never returned; Peter wanted to
walk round Amsterdam, and go to the cinema. For
Anne herself, 'most of all I long for a home of our own,
to be able to move freely, and to have some help with
my work again, in other words — school!' (4)

From time to time there was something to celebrate,
and then, for a day, everyone's spirits lifted. Birthdays
were never forgotten. The protectors were handed
secret shopping lists, as each birthday approached; and
the differences between Dr Dussel and the Van Daans
were drowned in a special bottle of wine, while Mrs
Van Daan brightened up over her pots of jam and
bouquet of red carnations. Anne had two birthdays in
the hiding place, and the number of presents she listed
for Kitty was astonishing. For her fifteenth birthday
she received eight books, some underwear, a hand-

kerchief, jam, yogurt, gingerbread, sweets, cream cheese, a bracelet, and a bunch of peonies.

Some of the Jewish festivals were observed; and, because the protectors were Christians, Christian festivals were observed too. Miep and Elli provided a basket of gifts for St Nicholas's Day in December 1942; and in 1943 Anne celebrated Christmas for the first time in her life, with a cake and special biscuits for everyone, and bottles of beer for the grown-ups. It was odd to do things differently, but it helped to break the monotony of the Secret Annexe.

Diary references
1. 23 August 1943
2. 24 August 1943
3. 16 September 1943
4. 23 July 1943

7   I Want to Write

It was August 7th 1943. Anne had been in hiding for over a year, and still there was no relief from the tensions of the Secret Annexe. By night there were air raids. By day the hiders were either quarrelling and scolding, or fussing over the fleas which Peter's cat, Mouschi, had brought in. Mr Koophuis scattered flea powder everywhere, but the hiders were sure there were fleas in their clothes, and they scratched incessantly.

Anne had to escape. She could not go out, but it was the weekend, and the offices were empty. Taking pen and paper, she ran downstairs, through the moving bookcase, and found a place where she could settle down to write in peace.

She imagined she was looking out of the window at a little girl playing in the yard below, a fair, blue-eyed girl, called — Kitty! What Anne wrote was more a description than a story. She pictured Kitty's daily life; she gave her a family of brothers and sisters, some pets, and an ambition to work in a factory among a lot of jolly, chattering girls. *Kitty*, as Anne called her narrative, was short and simple, but it proved again what her diary had already taught her. Writing was the best way of escaping from the Secret Annexe.

During the next week Anne began to write down memories of her school days. She described the teachers — prim Miss Riegel and explosive Mr Heesing — and the times she was in trouble for fooling about and gossiping. Through her diary she had learned to portray people and events in vivid words. She used this skill in the twenty stories and essays which were found with her diary in the hiding place.

But Anne's stories have more to them than just a lively style. They show that during the tedious months of 1943, something remarkable had been happening to her. She had been learning how to come to terms with her situation, and find good behind the troubles which overshadowed her.

Through clear, painful observations of herself and the other hiders, she had worked out a scale of values — what was right and what was wrong, what important and what unimportant — and she used these ideas in her stories. She did not just want to amuse her readers. She wanted to tell them how best to live.

The Wise Old Dwarf, which she wrote in April 1944, is a fairy tale about the difficulties of living with other people. An elf who is annoyingly bright and cheerful, and a dwarf who is always glum, are imprisoned together in a small cottage by the wise old dwarf of the title. They have to work out the best way of coping with the situation, just as the hiders did; and in the end they learn to accept each other.

Most of the stories show characters facing the sort of difficulties Anne faced. One has a heroine who is on bad terms with her mother. Another shows a girl who is terrified of air raids. Usually Anne finds a satisfactory solution. The stories are sad, but they are never just pessimistic.

A week after *The Wise Old Dwarf*, Anne wrote one of her favourite stories. *Blurry the Explorer* is about a teddy bear who runs away to discover the world. Everything is seen from teddy bear height — shoes, chair legs, car tyres — and Blurry is often puzzled and alarmed by the enormous things which get in his way. 'Did you discover the world?' his mother asks, when he finally returns home. 'No,' says Blurry, 'not really; you see, I couldn't find it!'

By 1944 Anne was beginning to think about what she might do when she grew up. In spite of the Nazis, she could not help hoping there would be some future for her. She believed that one day she would leave the Secret Annexe; and because, by then, she might be too old for school, she would have to be ready to earn her living. She was determined not just to be a housewife, like her mother and Mrs Van Daan. 'I must have something besides a husband and children, something I can devote myself to,' (1) she wrote.

She would, she decided, become a journalist. 'I know I can write,' she told Kitty. 'A couple of my stories are good, my descriptions of the Secret Annexe are humorous, there's a lot in my diary that speaks . . . If I haven't any talent for writing books and newspaper articles, well then I can always write for myself.' (2)

In her inmost self, a thrilling ambition was stirring. After the war, she would write a book based on her own experiences in hiding. She would call it *Het Achterhuis*, which is Dutch for the house behind, or the Secret Annexe.

As she considered her writing — the diary letters, the stories and essays, the fragment of a novel about a teenage girl, *Cady* — she felt a surge of excitement. She

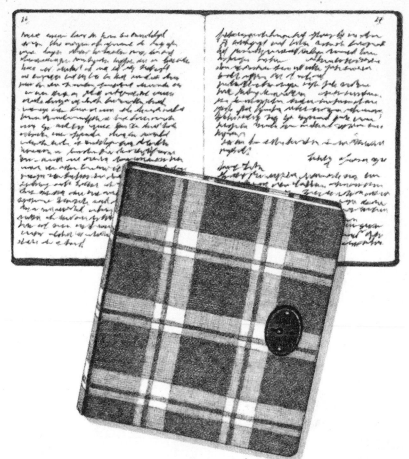

The Diary — open and closed

knew in her bones that it was good, and could bring her fame. 'I want to go on living after my death!' she exclaimed. 'I am grateful to God for giving me this gift . . . I can shake off everything if I write; my sorrows disappear, my courage is reborn . . . I think I shall succeed, because I want to write!' (3)

Diary references
1, 2, 3.   All 4 April 1944

8 Peter

While Anne was discovering the thrill of writing, something else was happening to her. She was falling in love.

Since the hiding began, Anne's nights had been times of torment — and not just from the tears, and the air raids, and the bullying of Dr Dussel. As she lay between sleeping and waking, terrible visions overwhelmed her. 'At night, when I'm in bed,' she told Kitty, 'I see myself alone in a dungeon, without Mummy and Daddy. Sometimes I wander by the roadside, or our Secret Annexe is on fire, or they come and take us away at night.' (1) Once her school friend, Lies, seemed to appear in the bedroom, ragged, thin and hollow-eyed from the horrors of the concentration camp where she was imprisoned. 'Help, oh help me,' she implored. 'Rescue me from this hell.' 'And I cannot help her,' wrote poor Anne. 'I can only pray to God to send her back to us.' (2)

The nightmares lasted for a year and a half, and then one night, quite unexpectedly, she had a very different dream. She thought she was looking at a book of drawings, and opposite her sat Peter Wessel, the boy she had loved in her school-days. She gazed into his eyes, and heard him say softly, 'If I had only known, I would have come to you long before.' (3) And he gently laid his cheek against hers.

The dream was a turning point for Anne. Peter's loving, ghostly presence seemed to bring some deep reassurance, some hope that, in the end, things would come right.

The dark clouds were indeed beginning to break. Through her stories, Anne had already found a way of escaping from the tensions around her; and often now, when she was not writing, she was thinking — struggling earnestly to find the right way of coping with problems like her unsympathetic mother. Most significantly, the dream came just at the moment when Anne's attention was beginning to focus for the first time on the teenage boy who shared the Secret Annexe. After all, he too was called Peter.

Until this point, Peter Van Daan had hardly mattered to Anne. Occasionally they had made fleeting contact, as when he had spilled the dried beans on her. But usually he was like Margot, 'staid and quiet' (4) as Anne put it.

Just before the dream, sheer loneliness had driven Anne to Peter's room. Her longing to talk to someone had become unbearable, and 'somehow or other,' she told Kitty, 'I took it into my head to choose Peter.' (5) She found, to her astonishment, that behind the quiet and apparently dull exterior, was a person very like herself. Peter too felt isolated, and desperately in need of a friend. Yet so far he had avoided the Franks. Compared with his parents, they seemed alarmingly clever. Daunted by the situation, he had shut himself away, pouring out all his affection on his cat, Mouschi. Anne decided that it was time she got to know him better.

She had to make several visits before the ice between them cracked. She talked to him, did crossword puzzles with him, and helped him to select the potatoes for supper. They began to understand each other; and, as they drew closer, friendship blossomed into love.

With her carefully curled hair, and lively dark eyes, Anne was a pretty girl. When she smiled there were dimples in her cheeks. Peter had been at school with her, and he remembered how people had clustered round her, and how she had been 'always laughing, always the centre of everything.' (6) Yet now it was not her looks and personality that appealed to him most. He loved her because she had chosen to be kind to him.

As for Anne, she decided that Peter was 'so handsome . . . such a darling, and so good.' (7) Even his shyness and clumsiness seemed attractive. At fourteen she was worldly wise and mature for her age. Peter was seventeen, but he seemed young and inexperienced. They felt themselves equals, united against the world.

After all their months of lonely misery, it was thrilling to discover how much they could share. 'We simply couldn't bear each other in the beginning,' Anne told Kitty. 'He thought I was much too talkative and unruly . . . I couldn't understand why he didn't flirt with me.' (8) Now she realized that there had not been much difference between her noise and his silence. Both had been ways of covering up unhappiness.

'I said I would love to help him,' Anne wrote. '"You always do help me," he said. "How?" I asked, very surprised. "By your cheerfulness" he replied.' (9) Anne thought that was the nicest thing he could have said. She knew that her boisterousness had been forgiven.

In the confines of the hiding place, their love grew stronger. Alone in Peter's bedroom they shared their first kiss. Evening after evening they sat quietly on his divan, their arms round each other, Anne's head on Peter's shoulder. Filled with peace and joy, they let their old troubles and anxieties sink into insignificance.

As night fell, Anne tore herself reluctantly away. It needed all her courage to go back to the living-room, and face the questions and laughter of the others. She only wanted to bury herself under the blankets, and dream in silence. Peter . . . Peter . . . At last she had found happiness in the Secret Annexe.

Diary references
1. 8 November 1943
2. 27 November 1943
3. 6 January 1944
4. 5 February 1943
5. 7 March 1944
6. 7 March 1944
7. 22 March 1944
8. 19 March 1944
9. 19 March 1944

9 Inward Compensations

Everything seemed to be coming right. Anne could look back over the dark months of hiding, and forward to the future, with a new composure. She had, she told Kitty, 'grown wise within these walls.' [1]

The days when she had kept up her courage with arguments and cheekiness were over. So were the nights when she had cried herself to sleep. She had discovered that there were ways of rising above the difficulties of her life. She had found what she called 'inward compensations.' [2]

Peter, and her writing, were two; but there were others. One was a new delight in nature.

From Peter's tiny room, a ladder-like staircase led to the loft, where sacks of vegetables, and other things, were stored. The window was so high that it did not need curtains, and Anne began to find immense happiness in just looking out. She forgot to envy the people down below. Instead she watched a chestnut tree, as it changed from winter bareness to full leaf. She gazed at the clouds and the birds, and the roofs of Amsterdam stretching to the blue horizon, and she no longer fretted because she could not go out. 'It's not imagination on my part,' she wrote, 'when I say that to

Otto Frank

look up at the sky, the clouds, the moon and stars, makes me calm and patient. It's a better medicine than valerian . . . Mother Nature makes me feel humble, and prepared to face every blow courageously.' (3)

As she watched the sky, or lay in bed, deep thoughts possessed her. She pondered on the personal problems of the Secret Annexe. Had they just been unlucky with Mr and Mrs Van Daan, she wondered. Would things have gone better with different people, or was some stress inevitable? Would her own life have been easier if her mother had been more sympathetic, or if Pim had listened to her troubles? She had felt so lonely before she got to know Peter; so neglected and misunderstood.

Now her self-pity had gone; and because she was so much happier, she made a new effort to understand the others. She found that even Mrs Van Daan had a sense of humour; that her mother quite genuinely believed her relationship with Anne was perfect; that Mr Van Daan and Dr Dussel could sometimes be generous; that Pim was a model of kindness and sensitivity. After making these discoveries there were still times when the other hiders got on Anne's nerves, but she bore it more patiently. She had learned to be independent of them.

A mixture of this new feeling of independence, and her love for Peter, caused an unexpected clash with her father. Pim had seldom joined in the scoldings Anne had received. He had remained aloof, and Anne had been grateful. So when he suddenly told her that she was growing too fond of Peter, and that she must not spend so much time alone with him, she was angry and astonished.

Thinking she could express herself best on paper, she wrote Pim a long letter. She explained to him how her inward struggles had finally made her strong. 'Now that I've fought the battle,' she told him, 'I want to be able to go on in my own way, the way I think is right. You can't and mustn't regard me as fourteen; these troubles have made me older.' (4) She refused to give Peter up.

Pim was deeply hurt by her disobedience. He told her so, and Anne was upset too. But somehow she won her point. Since her parents had not helped her when she needed them, they had lost their influence over her. It no longer really mattered what they thought. Anne went on visiting Peter, just as before.

The other inward compensation, which increased as

the months went by, was her faith in God. As the cause of the whole terrible situation was their Jewishness, Anne might well have resented being born a Jew. Peter certainly did. He hated his religion, and wanted to have nothing to do with it.

Anne did not agree. Religion was a source of strength to her. Although the Franks were not the kind of orthodox Jews who followed every rule of their faith, they had taught Anne to say her prayers, and she never forgot them. Every night she tried to entrust herself, her family and friends, into the hands of God.

God, she believed, was very close to her. 'God has not left me alone,' (5) she told Kitty; and 'God has never deserted our people.' (6) Belief in God meant trying to live the way God wanted. It meant loving people, however tiresome they were; it meant sharing good things, instead of clinging selfishly to them; it meant working for peace, in family relationships and in the world.

Such ideals really inspired Anne. She longed to be a better person. The world needed good people, if things were to be better after the war. Hundreds of years before Anne was born, the Jewish prophets of the Bible had seen visions of how God intended life to be. Anne read the Bible, and something of a prophet's fervour excited her as, in March 1944, she wrote her finest essay, *Give*.

'How lovely to think that no one need wait a moment, we can start now, start slowly changing the world! How lovely that everyone, great and small, can make their contribution towards introducing justice straight away

. . . Give of yourself, give as much as you can! And you can always give something, even if it is only kindness . . . Give and you shall receive, much more than you would ever have thought possible. Give, give again and again, don't lose courage, keep it up, and go on giving! No one has ever become poor from giving! . . . There is plenty of room for everyone in the world, enough money, riches and beauty for everyone to share. God has made enough for everyone! Let us begin then by sharing it fairly.'

Diary references
1. 7 March 1944
2. 23 February 1944
3. 15 June 1944
4. 5 May 1944
5. 31 March 1944
6. 11 April 1944

10 Not Forgotten

As the spring of 1944 dragged by, there were times
when Anne found it hard to keep up her cheerfulness.
In the world outside things seemed to be getting worse.
Hatred of the Jews, far from dying away, was as strong
as ever. Their protectors spoke of rumours that, when
the war was over, all the remaining Jews would be
thrown out of Holland.

The greengrocer who had secretly supplied them
with vegetables was arrested by the Gestapo. Already
food in the Secret Annexe was dull and restricted. Now
it became more limited, little more than porridge and
half rotten potatoes. Pim smiled wryly, remembering
his wealthy childhood, as he scraped the unappetizing
hash straight from the frying-pan onto the supper
plates.

The lavatory was blocked. The weather was too hot.
Somehow Peter, fond though he was of Anne, had not
developed into quite the understanding friend she had
hoped for. 'I feel so miserable,' she told Kitty. 'I haven't
felt like this for months.' (1)

Ten days later her mood changed dramatically. The
invasion of Europe had at last begun. British and
American troops landed in France, and began pushing
the Germans back. 'Oh Kitty!' Anne exclaimed, 'I have
the feeling that friends are approaching. We have been
oppressed by those terrible Germans for so long.' (2)
Hope soared in the Secret Annexe. Soon the war would
be over. 'Everything's all right here, and tempers are

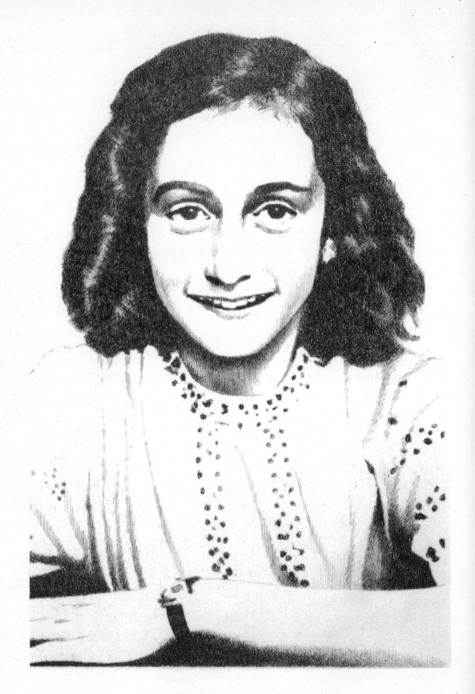

improving,' (3) Anne reported joyfully, as the advance of the Allies continued.

The end of the ordeal seemed to be in sight. Back in November 1943, Anne had painted a desolate picture of their plight. 'I see the eight of us with our Secret Annexe as if we were a little piece of blue heaven, surrounded by heavy black rain clouds. The round, clearly defined place where we stand is still safe, but the clouds gather more closely about us, and the circle which separates us from the approaching danger closes more and more tightly.' (4) Now the black circle seemed to be receding, and the prospect of going back to school in October made Anne feel light-headed with happiness.

'Little bundle of contradictions!' (5) she scolded herself. Why was she sometimes dizzy with hope, and sometimes utterly despondent? Once again she tried to explain herself to Kitty. She had, she decided, a dual personality. There was the lively, high-spirited self which she presented to the world, and the deeply reflective self which she had so far hidden. But it was the second self which really counted. She longed to show it to the world, but, when she tried, nobody took her seriously. As far as the other hiders were concerned, Anne was the last person to be idealistic and philosophical. She could not explain how she had 'grown wise within these walls'; how she wished her good self to develop, and her giddy self to disappear. She summed up her problem in the last words of the diary. 'I keep on trying to find a way of becoming what I would so like to be, and what I could be, if — there weren't any other people living in the world.' (6)

Three days later, on Friday, August 4th, a car drew up outside the warehouse. A German sergeant and four Dutch plain clothes policemen got out. What had made them suspicious of the old house by the canal was never revealed. Perhaps the greengrocer had betrayed something.

The sergeant ordered Mr Kraler to take them round the premises. When they reached the swinging bookcase, with its box files, he pulled out his revolver. Mr Kraler, the kind protector, had the bitter task of delivering the Jews to their enemies.

During all the time they had been in the Secret Annexe, the hiders had never devised an escape route. But perhaps there would not have been time to use it. With the revolver against his back, Mr Kraler climbed the stairs behind the bookcase, and opened the living-room door. 'The Gestapo is here,' he said quietly.

The nightmare moment had arrived. Sick with fear, the hiders were unable to put up any resistance. Anne stood motionless as the Secret Annexe was ransacked. She saw her diary and stories tossed to the floor, and the pitiful collection of valuables dropped into her briefcase. Then the eight Jews were taken out to the police van. They were driven away, along the canal and over the bridge, to the Gestapo headquarters.

Mr Kraler and Mr Koophuis were arrested too, but their lives were spared. Fortunately the Nazis never knew that Miep and Elli had been in the secret.

The Franks, the Van Daans and Dr Dussel were sent in a locked train to the Dutch camp at Westerbork. After their years inside, the journey seemed strangely

Children in one of Hitler's concentration camps

like a holiday; it was so wonderful to see the countryside again.

That was the last pleasure they knew. The families were separated, and sent to different concentration camps in Germany and Poland. Margot and Anne together went to Belsen. In February 1945, typhus fever swept the camp. Weakened by starvation, both sisters caught the disease. Margot died first; and Anne, who had until then showed tremendous courage, lived only a few days longer. Their mother had already died far away. Mr Frank, alone of all the hiders, survived, to be freed by the Russian army. He returned to Holland, where Miep and Elli gave him Anne's precious diary.

'I want to go on living, even after my death,' [7] Anne had written. She had guessed, rightly, that immortality could come through her writing. In 1947 her diary was published in Holland, and caused a sensation. Quickly it was translated into other languages, and sold all over the world. Millions of people read the letters to Kitty, and shared with Anne the joys and sorrows of the Secret Annexe. The book was adapted for films, television and the theatre. It was read on the radio, and studied in schools. Anne's stories and essays were published too, in a book called *Tales from the House Behind.*

Why did the diary of a Jewish teenager win such fame? The chief reason was the personality it revealed, a personality full of courage, sensitivity and goodness. 'I shall not remain insignificant', [8] Anne had told Kitty; and her confidence was justified. She has not been forgotten.

Diary references
1. 26 May 1944
2.   6 June 1944
3. 30 June 1944
4.   8 November 1943
5.   1 August 1944
6.   1 August 1944
7.   4 April 1944
8. 11 April 1944